HOW TO EARN MONEY
WITH YOUR BLOG IN 2019

LEARN HOW TO GENERATE INCOME ONLINE STEP BY
STEP, GENERATE THOUSANDS OF VISITS TO YOUR
WEBSITE, BECOME A EXPERT BLOGGER

Gaston Echevarria

First Edition

Table of Contents

Introduction

Want to make money in the world of profitable blogging? Are you looking forward to becoming one of those 6-figure bloggers you've heard so much about?

If so, you'll want to read every word of this special report because I'm going to show you exactly how you can join the ranks of those who have cultivated regular buyer tracking through a network of highly targeted blogs.

I've eliminated the clutter and wasted time so I can get you to the heart of successful blogs without complicating the process too much, or forcing you to go through a long, drawn-out learning curve.

Because the truth is, it doesn't have to be that complicated.

Making money with carefully designed niche blogs is not so hard to do. In fact, if you are looking for a quick and easy way to set up the store so you can start making money online without a big investment, blogging is the way to go.

Creating high-quality blogs in your niche or industry that generate traffic and provide valuable content and information to your market is also one of the most effective methods to build an authoritative presence and establish yourself within your industry, plus incredible profit margins; blogs put you in a great position within your market.

And guess what? The best part of this strategy is that it is also exceptionally easy to do and very cost effective. It doesn't cost much money to create a blog. In fact, most work will involve your time - not your dollars.

So, without further ado, let's start at once!

Can you make a lot of money with blogs?

Here's the truth about six-figure blogs: While blogs can (eventually) be automated, you shouldn't expect revenues to be passive from the start. You'll have to work on it, especially when you're launching your blog and building a platform that you want to be recognized in your market.

When I started blogging I spent 30-50 hours a month creating content, turning visitors into email subscribers and selling products and services (none of which I created myself - I focused entirely on affiliate marketing. More about that later).

While I eventually outsourced most of

my content to expert writers, I still spend time evaluating advertising options, reviewing the products I can promote, building my mailing list and creating advertising campaigns to increase traffic and keep my blogs at the forefront.

While you can delegate many tasks to a team, such as content creation and even marketing, you'll want to be directly involved in the initial phase of construction. This is your brand, after all. You need to make sure that every piece of content has your voice, carries your message and represents your business in the best possible way.

No one will ever be as careful and professional with building your blog as you are, right? So, keep your heels and commit to spending the first few months of building your blog from the ground floor up. Then, and only then, should you start creating a team that will help you manage your blog and eventually expand to other avenues with other niche-based blogs (if you decide to do that).

Again, blogging is by no means a hands-free method for making money during the INITIAL stages. You must be prepared to put in some time and effort if you really want to succeed.

But the good news? Your hard work will pay off.

The best ways to make money with your blog

While there are countless reports and articles that over-complicated the process of making money from blogging, here's a basic summary of how it's done:

1: Create a blog and register a memorable domain. Avoid remotely hosted options. You need to have full control of your website so you can take advantage of all the different income options without limitations (or other people's ads).

2: Write (or outsource) content that generates traffic and attracts visitors. This content must be of high quality, specific and informative. All meat, no vegetables.

3: Turn your visitors into email subscribers so you can create your list. A newsletter is key in building a successful online blog. Scratch that; a newsletter is essential to succeed in almost any online marketplace. You'll never make that much money without one.

4: Communicate with those subscribers regularly so their lists don't get cold. Build a relationship of communication and trust. Encourage relationships with your market. This is where you can build a brand recognized as an authority in your market and differentiate yourself from the competition (especially from those bloggers who aren't doing this!).

5: Sell products and services to your audience through your blog and your newly cultivated newsletter.

Sounds pretty easy, doesn't it? It is. But it will take time. Let's go a little deeper into each of these steps so you can better understand how it works.

➢ CREATE YOUR BLOG

This report focuses on how to make money with your blog, so I won't go into details about building the platform. Just know that you should always choose a memorable domain that targets your market and that you set up a professional hosting account that contains your blog. Do not use a free host or remote hosting option such as Blogger.

➢ CREATE CONTENT FOR YOUR BLOG

The type of content you create will depend on your target audience, but each piece of content should always be informative and the most juicy and relevant topic you can think of.

Your content will be what drives traffic and keeps visitors coming back to your blog. You need to establish your blog as an informative source of content in your marketplace, so be sure to spend more time developing compelling content (or outsourcing to experienced writers who know your market inside and out).

Internal tip: An easy way to provide additional value on your website is to use a plugin such as www.PostGopher.com that will convert the content of your article into PDF files that your visitors can save on their computers. This allows them to read it later, keeping their attention and increasing their chances of digesting its content.

➢ *BUILD AND CONVERT CUSTOMERS*

You need to be always working to build your list. This is a process that you can set up on autopilot using onsite opt-in forms that capture visitor information and add it to your mailing list. Plugins such as www.OptinMonster.com make it easy to add visitors to your mailing lists.

Offer an incentive to those who join your lists, such as providing them with a special report not available anywhere else on your blog, or special offers and discounts on products and services. You always have to deliver more than you need and start carefully. Don't flood your subscribers with paid offers right away - establish a relationship with them first and let them know you're looking out for their interests.

Then, set up autoresponder campaigns that will transmit a variety of valuable, free offers to your subscribers over time. I personally set up an introductory and welcome email to send my subscribers as soon as they join my list.

Then, 2-3 days later, I have another automated email that offers a free special report on my niche. Then, a week later, I start conditioning them to open my emails because they know they will get value for doing so. Another free offer, a special discount code or a special infograph based on what most interests my visitors.

It's not until 7-12 days later before I start selling actively, and I do it as passively as possible. Instead of bold and face-to-face offers, I work WITH them by providing them with valuable resources or tools that I believe will help or improve their lives in some way.

When subscribers feel that you are a friend taking care of them, rather than a seller whose only interest is to make money, they will respond accordingly. So, don't be an aggressive email marketer - be a professional blogger with a pulse in your market and one who is willing to go the distance for your visitor (and potential customers).

> ### *Earn their trust and respect.*

And finally, sell products and services as if it were nobody's business! That's when you'll start earning money with your blog and, as you do, you'll see what your visitors are responding to so you can adjust your system and start adapting both your email campaigns and the content of your blog, depending on what interests them most.

Which brings us to the essence of this report: HOW to make money.

What products or services should you sell? How can you turn free content into profit? How can you use your blog as a lead generation tool that allows you to earn money on a consistent basis?

I'll show you how in the next chapter.

Affiliates!

One of the most important aspects of building a profitable blog is deciding which form of monetization will work best for your market.

There are many different options available to you, so figuring out which one to start with (and ultimately calibrating which format your visitors are most likely to respond to) is often the most complicated part of the process.

So let's break it down so that you can create a secure system that will allow you to earn money in no time, avoiding the low yield options that so many people are victims of.

DEFINE YOUR OBJECTIVE:

You can start a blog simply because you are interested in writing content for your niche market. Maybe you have a lot of information to share and enjoy helping others. Great! But, you still need to define the purpose of your blog.

Is your blog designed to attract visitors with useful and free content that you can turn into an advantage?

Are you planning to use your blog to offer a free offer in exchange for an email address to create specific mailing lists?

If so, then your blog is a mechanism for generating potential customers and that is your goal.

The goal of creating a blog is not just to make money selling products and services directly, either with your own offers or through affiliate marketing offers. Your blog should also be a tool for generating potential customers, a way to enter your market, and build authority in your niche.

So *how should you start monetizing your blog?*

> ➤ ***Affiliate Marketing!***

Even if you have a product or service of your own, if you are new to your niche and are not established as a product developer, you should start by creating compelling content for your blog and monetizing that content with established products and services from business owners who offer affiliate marketing options.

You can then siphon the credibility of these established professionals, and better yet, you can let them do most of the work!

With affiliate marketing, you're not stuck at desktops supporting the emails of customers who need help.

You are not working with graphic designers, promotional material and media kits to provide tools for promoters to use.

You are not working on product updates, chasing and repairing problems or bugs in your software.

As an affiliate, you have a job to do: Sell

the product and earn money!

Affiliate marketing is definitely the smartest strategy.

> ### ➢ *Do you need more conviction?*

Affiliate marketers can set up profitable blogs faster than anyone else because you are not spending months investing time and money in product creation. You can choose from hundreds of high-performance products and present them on your blog with just a few clicks.

Affiliate marketers can generate income that is almost purely passive. You are not involved in support, development or updates, which leaves you free to create content, create your email lists and evaluate the developer's products that will make you as much money as possible.

And affiliate marketing can also introduce you to hot selling products, giving you ideas for your own product later on the road once your blog is set up and you are generating constant traffic! You'll know exactly what type of products you sell without having to extensively test your own products, minimizing the risk of failure.

It's a win-win situation.

The only exception to this rule is if you are a service provider. If you make money offering consulting, selling real estate or any other type of service, you'll want to start offering those services on your blog from the beginning. But if you're not a service provider, affiliate marketing is the only monetization strategy you should focus on.

This is what you must sell...

If you are thinking, "What kind of affiliate products should I sell? That's the only thing to worry about when choosing how to monetize your blog.

The key to success is not going after cheap markets. Don't make the mistake of thinking it's better to sell a $10 product because more people are likely to buy it. It's not true, it's not logical. In fact, you'll make things harder for yourself and have to work much harder to generate a decent income each month.

Instead, do what professional bloggers do: start with high-end affiliate products ($77 and up) and go down. Not only will you earn more money, but you won't have to sell almost as many copies to do it!

The only way a low-end product will work is if you have a solid backing of higher-priced products. In the edition, the authors call this first product (book 1 of its series) a lost leader. Basically, you're selling at a price low enough to qualify buyers (rather than free search engines), while seducing them into buying your higher-priced backend products. That's where you make your money.

In affiliate marketing, the only way to sell an initial offer at a low price makes sense if you have a series of high-priced back end offers to grab. When you start blogging (and in affiliate marketing), it's much easier to go for gold and promote higher-priced deals on your front, while cutting your teeth in the process.

In addition, as you promote affiliate offers and create your email lists, you can easily launch your own product later at a higher price because you have cultivated groups of subscribers who feel comfortable paying higher prices.

And remember, the metric that is above all others is the number on your mailing list. Don't worry about subscribers to RSS feeds - which are no longer worth considering - just focus on building your newsletters, as that will be the true predictor of how much money your blog will make.

WHAT YOU NEED TO KNOW:

How can you find the best affiliate products for your blog?

The easiest solution is to join Chitika's

advertising network here:
https://chitika.com/publishers

While there are many different ad networks (and I will share with you some others that make money in a moment), Chitika is one of the main online ad networks.

Here are some others I've used. These are all fantastic resources for new blogs:

LinkShare: *Rakuten Marketing:

<font color=#38B0DE>-=https://www.linkshare.com/=- Proudly Presents

One of the largest online affiliate networks with over 10 million affiliate associations. You will not be short of choices of products and services to choose from.

Commission Junction:

<font color=#38B0DE>-
=http://www.cj.com/=- Proudly Presents

This is the one I started with many years ago (I even have a wooden train whistle they sent to their first wave of affiliates), and I still use it today. Very reliable and reliable advertising network.

ShareASale:

<font color=#38B0DE>-
=https://www.shareasale.com/=- Proudly Presents

One of the most popular advertising networks with more than 3,000 merchants participating, so you'll find a ton of products to promote.

Amazon Affiliate Program:

<font color=#38B0DE>-=https://affiliate-program.amazon.com/=- Proudly Presents

Although the payment ratio is lower than many other networks, they offer you the ability to sell products from a highly recognized brand, in addition to having access to your entire product inventory. I recommend trying a handful of products when you start writing on your blog, as they are exceptionally easy to use.

I will include some of the other advertising networks that I have used at the end of this report in the resources section. For now, join these four networks and scan your inventory for a handful of products that are relevant to your niche and what you think your visitors would be most interested in.

Then create your content. If you have a

tight budget and plan to outsource most of the work, spend most of your money on content development. That's how you'll stand out from other blogs in your market, capture the attention of your audience and encourage repeat traffic. If you don't do anything else, spend time (or money) to create KILLER content of the highest possible quality.

➢ *Not sure what to write about?*

Research the top 10 blogs in your niche market. Look at what they're writing, what kind of headlines and titles they're using. Which articles get the most tastes and comments? Write down everything you find, creating an information slider that will help you create the type of content that most interests those in your market.

Take your time with this! If you're not sure what kind of content your visitors want most, you really need to spend some time researching before you start. It doesn't take long. Spend an hour or two scanning popular blogs and you'll quickly have a list of possible ideas.

Remember, all you really need to start blogging is 2-3 high quality items. Or, turn the script around and offer your visitors a combination of content types, including infographics, articles, or a video.

And always set up your opt-in mailing list before you start directing traffic to your blog.

If you want an affordable option that's also easy to use, visit http://www.MailerLite.com or http://www.MailChimp.com and then integrate an opt-in application such as LeadPages.net or OptinMonster.com to streamline the process.

Recap:

- Create 2-5 pieces of killer content in the form of articles, infographs, or videos.

- Invest in a mailing list service and set up your welcome/presentation email. Do not sell in the first 2-3 emails.

- Offer them ONE thing for free: a report, a free download, or something else that appeals to your market.

- Integrate 1-3 affiliate products into your blog content and mailing list newsletters.

- When you can afford it, buy an opt-in plug-in for mailing lists that captures potential customers.

You can do without this by simply incorporating your mailing list registration code into your own blog, but honestly, applications like OptinMonster.com are much more professional, as they will not only automatically create pop-ups or site forms, but you can also customize them to appear based on the user's activity (for example, how many times the visitor has been there, where the visitor is on your website, etc.).

- Evaluate affiliate products regularly from within affiliate networks. Keep the pulse on your market by constantly visiting blogs set up in your niche in order to keep up with the type of content you are getting a lot of attention as well as the type of products you are selling.

 - Generate traffic! Engage potential visitors through social media, create advertising campaigns with Google's content viewing network, use forums and communities within your niche to present your blog and maximize exposure.

Conclusion

I want you to start selling today. Don't make the mistake so many novice bloggers make and think you should first increase your subscriber list to 1,000 before you start selling. Don't worry about having "enough" content on your blog.

Start by publishing 2-3 highly informative articles on your blog that will be of interest to your target audience and choose from 1 to 3 affiliate products to promote. Divide that and present a product for every 2-3 articles on your blog, with the other affiliate offers that are sent to your newsletter subscribers.

The key is not to be insistent. Provide valuable content that attracts visitors and integrates one or two affiliate offerings into your blog structure. In this way, you are not putting it in their face, but rather reminding them of a useful tool or service that will help them in some way.

It's hard to stay motivated as a blogger if you're not making money, so if you start your efforts immediately, instead of trying to perfect everything, you'll see results much faster. You can also generate revenue that will go towards training your team, hiring writers and marketing professionals.

Once you've cashed that first check or accepted that first Paypal payment for your affiliate sales, trust me; you'll be hooked.

Now yes, I wish you the best in your results, and remember, everything is practical; theory without action is of no use to you.

A big hug, your friend, Gaston!

By the way, when you achieve your results little by little, I highly recommend you, if you want to learn much more about methods of making money, my book, on "MAKING MONEY WITH YOUR INSTAGRAM ACCOUNT", is a book that I am sure will help you a lot on your way to "financial freedom". Without further ado, you can find it in the Amazon search engine, like: "Make money with your instagram account" or looking for my name, like: "Gaston Echevarria"... Once again I wish you success in your results!

Extra resources

Campaign Resources

Here are links to the resources found in this guide:

Advertising networks:

LinkShare: https://www.linkshare.com/

Commission Junction:
http://www.cj.com/

ShareASale:
https://www.shareasale.com/

Amazon Partner Program:
https://affiliate-program.amazon.com/

Google Affiliate Network:
https://www.google.com/ads/affiliatenetw
ork/

Top Choice for Digital Products:
www.JVZoo.com

Professional tip: Provide added value by turning your content into downloadable PDF forms that your visitors will love! == sync, corrected by <font color="#00ff00">elderman == == for <font color="#00ffff">http://www.PostGopher.com ==

Optional forms/list builders:

http://www.OptinMonster.com

http://www.LeadPages.net

Mailing list providers:

http://www.mailerlite.com

http://www.MailChimp.com

www.ingramcontent.com/pod-product-compliance
Lightning Source LLC
Chambersburg PA
CBHW071445170526
45158CB00005BA/1836

* 9 7 8 1 0 9 0 3 5 8 0 8 0 *